Native Pride
in the Americas and Australia

Carol Ghiglieri

A Harcourt Achieve Imprint

www.Steck-Vaughn.com
1-800-531-5015

Native Pride in the Americas and Australia
By Carol Ghiglieri

Photo Acknowledgements
Cover ©Alison Wright/CORBIS; p. 10–11 ©Bettman/CORBIS; p. 12 ©Layne Kennedy/CORBIS; p. 14–15 ©Ludo Kuipers, OzOutback Internet Services; p. 16–17 ©Penny Tweedie/CORBIS; p. 21 ©Raimund Franken/Peter Arnold, Inc.; p. 27 ©Dario Lopez-Mills/AP Wide World Photos; p. 29 ©Gregg Newton/Reuters/Newscom.

ISBN 1-4190-2288-1

© 2007 Harcourt Achieve Inc.

All rights reserved. No part of the material protected by this copyright may be reproduced or utilized in any form or by any means, in whole or in part, without permission in writing from the copyright owner. Requests for permission should be mailed to: Paralegal Department, 6277 Sea Harbor Drive, Orlando, FL 32887.

Steck-Vaughn is a trademark of Harcourt Achieve Inc.

Printed in the United States of America
1 2 3 4 5 6 7 8 152 12 11 10 09 08 07 06 05

Table of Contents

Introduction
Culture Clash 4

Chapter One
A Bloody History 6
   "Why Not Sell the Air?" 13

Chapter Two
Eddie Mabo's Fight 14
   Dreamtime 20

Chapter Three
The Tribe That Hides from Man 22
   Shrinking Forests 28

Glossary 30

Index 32

Introduction

Culture Clash

For thousands of years, **thriving** cultures existed in Australia, North America, and Central America. People farmed, hunted, or gathered food. The Incas, Aztecs, and Maya built huge empires in Central America. Yet, none of these **indigenous** cultures had any knowledge of European societies across the oceans. Meanwhile, Europeans had no knowledge of the American and Australian continents.

In the 15th century, all that began to change. European explorers set off across the Atlantic, then

later across the Pacific. Settlers followed soon after. Europeans began to **colonize** the Caribbean. They also started colonies in South America and North America. Finally, in 1788, they came to Australia, too.

The colonists brought guns and disease. They needed land for farms and ranches. And they weren't afraid to take it. Life for the indigenous people would never be the same.

Today, their descendants are fighting for their rights and struggling to save their cultures. This book is about three of those struggles.

- **In the 15th century, the Spanish began settling the Caribbean islands and Central America.**
- **In the 16th century, Portuguese explorers arrived in South America.**
- **In the 17th century, the British arrived in North America to stay.**
- **In the 18th century, British settlers began to colonize Australia.**

Chapter One

A Bloody History

European settlers arrived in North America in the early 1600s. The continent was already home to about 10 million American Indians. Europeans first settled on the East Coast, then pushed west. In 1830, Congress passed the Indian Removal Act. This law began the policy of **relocation**. Soldiers forced thousands of American Indians in the East off their own land. The tribes settled in a dry area west of the Mississippi River known as Indian Territory. Over the next 50 years, American Indians in the West were also forced to move. Soldiers herded them onto assigned areas called **reservations**.

Many tribes put up **resistance**. The result was decades of violence. These tribes eventually fought more than 1,000 battles to keep their land.

Many of these wars ended in a similar way. Tribal chiefs signed treaties with the U.S. government. The treaties drew new borders between "Indian country" and U.S. land. Indian country got smaller and smaller.

For years, the Sioux were lucky. They lived on the Great Plains. Their land was dry and rocky. Few whites wanted to settle there. An 1851 treaty protected their land. Then, in the 1860s, miners discovered gold in Montana. More miners poured through Sioux hunting grounds. War broke out.

Land Grab

These maps show the land lost by Native Americans between 1775 and 1894.

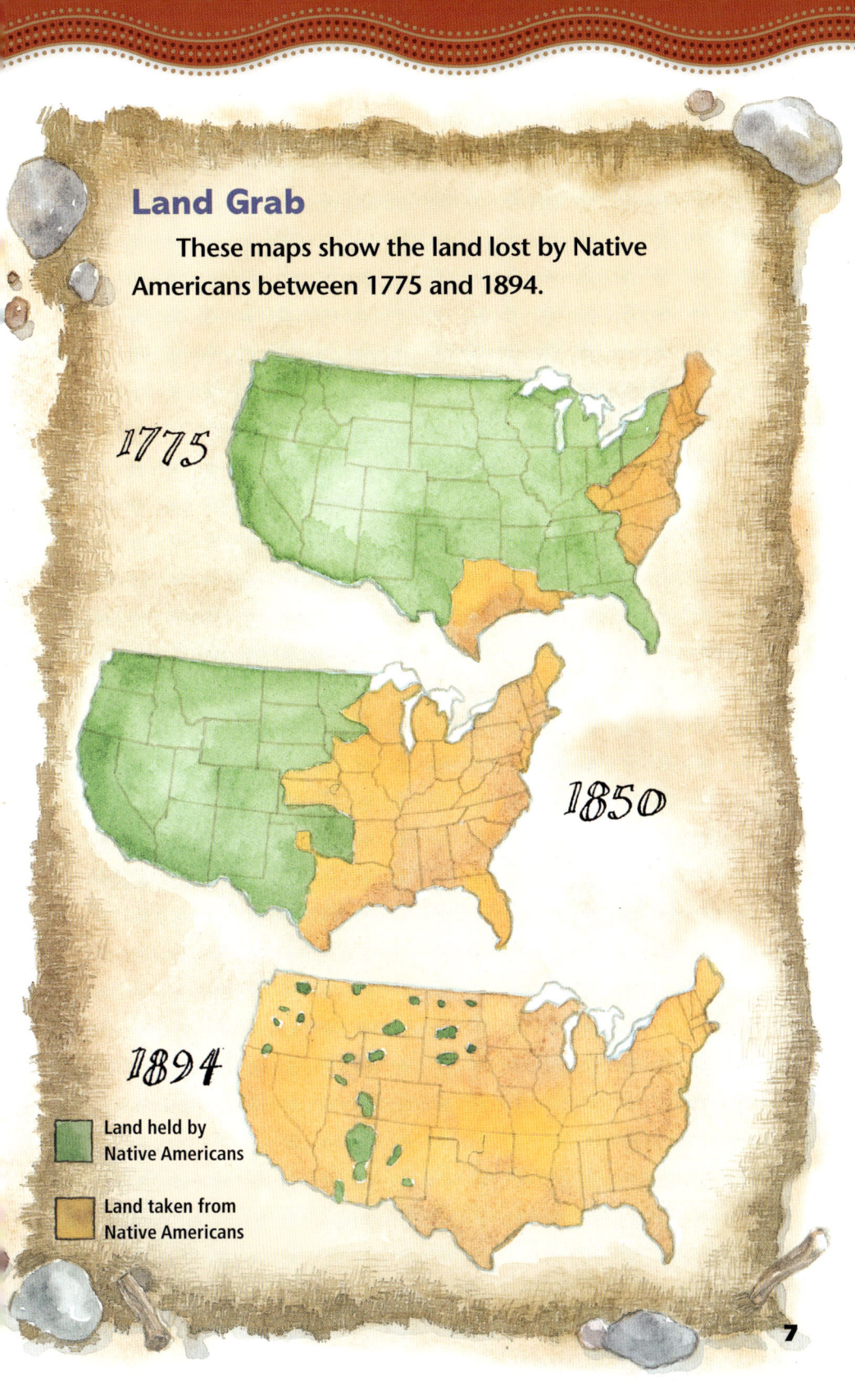

1775

1850

1894

Land held by Native Americans

Land taken from Native Americans

In 1868, the Sioux signed a new treaty at Fort Laramie, Wyoming. When gold was found there, however, that treaty was violated, too.

Over the next 20 years, nearly all the Sioux were moved to reservations. The buffalo they once hunted were almost extinct. The old way of life was gone.

In 1890, the U.S. army thought the Sioux were planning a revolt. That December, soldiers arrested 350 Lakota Sioux. They wanted the Lakota to turn over their weapons. A shot went off. The soldiers started firing. When they were through, more than 150 Lakota were dead. The camp where they died was on Wounded Knee Creek.

Youth Movement

In the 1960s, American Indians started protesting again. In 1968, a group called the American Indian Movement (AIM) was formed. AIM had a long list of **grievances**. They wanted the U.S. government to give them more freedom. They felt that American Indians had lost much of their culture on reservations. So, AIM members often wore traditional dress.

In January 1973, AIM added another complaint. It was the murder of a Lakota named Wesley Bad Heart Bull. Bad Heart Bull was stabbed to death by a white man. Yet the attacker served just two months in prison.

To many Sioux, this was a terrible injustice. They claimed the courts had a **bias** against Native Americans. "It meant another Indian killer would go free," said one woman.

At this time, Wounded Knee was part of the Pine Ridge Reservation. The Oglala Sioux made their home there. They are a part of the Lakota tribe. Pine Ridge was one of the poorest places in the country. Most reservations weren't much wealthier. The jobless rate stood at 10 times the national average. Health care on reservations remained poor. The average Native American died at the age of 44. The average American lived until the age of 75. It was all too much for AIM to accept.

A month after Bad Heart Bull's murder, AIM and some other Sioux men took over Wounded Knee. Federal troops quickly moved in to stop them. The soldiers carried machine guns and drove armored trucks. They blocked the roads. AIM supporters had to sneak supplies into Wounded Knee in backpacks.

Russell Means was AIM's spokesman, and he was angry. He hoped Wounded Knee would make the government stand up and listen. Native Americans lived in **inferior** conditions. Many had no jobs. Nearly 40 percent lived in poverty. Means felt the government supported **corrupt** tribal leaders. Native Americans, he said, needed more control over their own lives.

One morning, Means listened to the radio. **Federal** troops had surrounded the village. Means turned to a friend. "We probably won't get out of this alive," he said.

The days wore on. The two sides traded gunfire. Near the end of April, the standoff turned deadly. An FBI agent shot an AIM member. He died on April 25. The next day, gunfire killed another Sioux man.

The takeover of Wounded Knee turned into a ten-week standoff. It was the first major conflict between U.S. troops and American Indians in 80 years. It reminded Americans that a long and troubled story was far from over.

Finally, President Richard Nixon agreed to look into the Native Americans' complaints. On May 8, the standoff ended. It had lasted 71 days.

Unfortunately, the protest at Wounded Knee did not change much. Many people at Pine Ridge still live in poverty. More than two-thirds of the residents have no jobs. Over one in four have no homes. Much work remains in helping Native Americans improve their conditions.

A young AIM member named Crow Dog applies war paint to the face of Russell Means at Wounded Knee. The town was surrounded by FBI agents and U.S. Marshals.

Yet, Native Americans are finding ways to move ahead. Court decisions have given them more control over tribal lands. Some tribes have opened **casinos**. Some sell traditional jewelry and other crafts on the Internet. These businesses bring in money for the tribes. These successes may also owe something to the struggle at Wounded Knee.

According to Russell Means, the siege gave Native Americans a new sense of dignity and pride. That pride, he says, "continues to this very day."

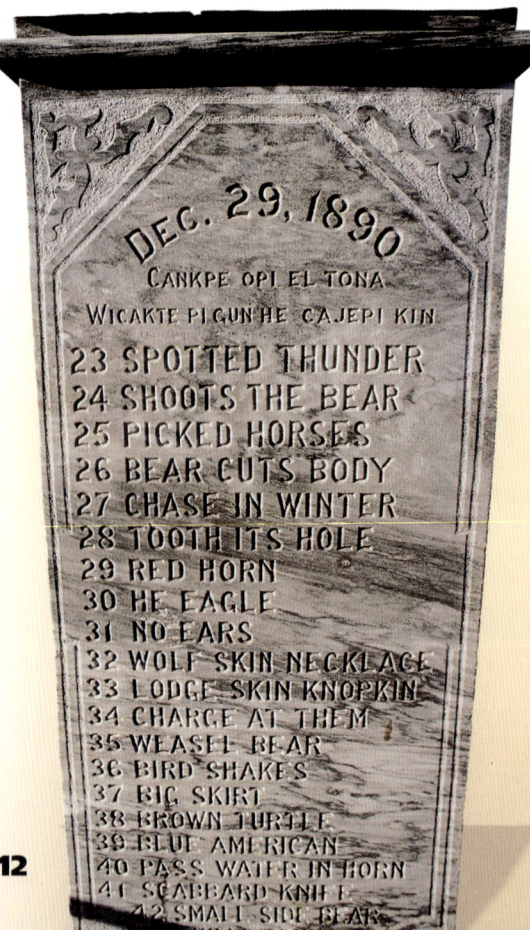

This monument stands in the cemetary at Wounded Knee. It recognizes many Native Americans who died there in the struggle for their rights.

"Why Not Sell the Air?"

Tecumseh was a leader of the Shawnee tribe. In the early 1800s, he fought American troops in the Ohio Valley. In 1810, he made this speech to Ohio governor William Henry Harrison. He explained that the land is for everyone to share. His words still carry an important message today.

You are continually driving the red people [off of their land].... At last you will drive them into the great lake [Lake Michigan], where they can neither stand nor work.

The red people [must] unite in claiming a common and equal right in the land, as it was at first, and should be now—for it was never divided, but belongs to all.

No tribe has the right to sell, even to each other, much less to strangers.

Sell a country?! Why not sell the air, the great sea, as well as the earth? Did not the Great Spirit make them all for the use of his children?

Chapter Two

Eddie Mabo's Fight

Eddie Mabo wanted to visit his father. His dad lay dying on Mer Island, a small island off the coast of Australia in the Torres (TOR-iz) Strait. The year was 1973.

Eddie lived on the mainland. In his heart, though, Mer would always be Eddie's home. He had grown up there. His ancestors had lived there for thousands of years. He felt a great **loyalty** to his

people. Now, the Australian government wouldn't let him go back. Eddie had been fighting for the rights of indigenous people. The government didn't want him making trouble on Mer.

Empty Land?

For thousands of years, people had lived in small groups all across the Australian mainland and on nearby islands. We know them now as **Aborigines** (ab-o-RIJ-i-nees). Three centuries ago, Eddie Mabo's ancestors had never seen a white person. Few people in that part of the world had.

Eddie Mabo's home, Mer Island, lies just off the northeast coast of Australia.

In the 1780s, English settlers arrived in Australia. They claimed the land for England. In 1879, they claimed the Torres Islands, too. When the British first arrived, there were 750,000 Aborigines living in Australia. Most were **nomadic**. They moved around in search of food. They didn't stay in one place to farm or build on the land. So the British settlers used a law known as *terra nullius*. That's Latin for "empty land." It meant that under British law, no one owned the land. It was free for the taking.

The colonists moved in fast. They brought deadly diseases to Australia. Aborigines had no defense against the germs. Many of them died. Others were pushed out of their homelands. They were forced to settle on dry, dusty patches of land.

The British settlers didn't move onto Mer Island. So, life for the islanders didn't change as much. They fished and gathered food just as they had for centuries. Their traditions passed along from generation to generation.

Aboriginal Australians protest for fair treatment in their homeland. They want land returned to them.

Still, they were a **minority** in a mostly white country. The islanders had to follow British laws. Eddie Mabo saw these laws in action as he grew up. Islanders couldn't **testify** in court. They weren't allowed to vote. The government controlled wages. It could keep whites and Aborigines from marrying each other. Eddie knew the situation wasn't fair.

As a teenager, Eddie went to the mainland. He got a job as a gardener at a university. Eddie was asked to lecture in class about life on Mer. He began teaching about his people and their customs.

Before long, Eddie became active in politics. He joined groups that were fighting for aboriginal rights. He spoke in public. He opened a special school for indigenous kids. He wanted his people to hold on to their language and culture. "We need to teach these things to our children," Eddie said. "We need to keep our songs and stories alive."

In the 1960s, indigenous people won the right to vote in Australia. Eddie knew this was important, but it wasn't enough.

Whose Land Is It, Anyway?

After his father died, Eddie wanted to get back to Mer. The government refused to let him. Eddie went anyway. He loved the island. It had rich soil and bamboo forests. It had palm trees and sandy beaches. To him, it was **paradise**.

Back on the mainland, he told his friends about the trip. He owned a nice piece of land. He could garden and fish. He could watch the sun set over the water. Someday, he would go back.

One day, Eddie was speaking to a teacher at the university. "That land isn't *your* land," the teacher **informed** him. "It belongs to Australia, not you." According to Australian law, the teacher was right. Thanks to *terra nullius*, Eddie had no right to his family's land. He was stunned.

In 1982, Eddie sued the Australian government. He claimed that the land on Mer was his. He argued that the government of Australia had stolen the land from the Aborigines.

The courts **debated** the issue for ten years. Eddie didn't live to hear the court's decision. In January 1992, he died of cancer. Five months later, the court ruled that Eddie had been right. The land did not belong to the Australian government. It belonged to the people of Mer Island.

Eddie Mabo's victory changed Australian law. The ruling allowed native people to sue for the rights to land they lost long ago. In Mer, Eddie is remembered as a hero. Three and a half years after his death, he finally went home for good. His body was flown back to Mer. He was buried not far from the land that now belongs to his family.

Dreamtime

Thousands of years ago, Aboriginal artists created some of the earliest known paintings. They painted on rocks. They painted on cave walls. Sometimes, they painted on human bodies. They didn't think of their work as art, though. They never thought of selling it. The paintings were part of their religion.

Today, Aboriginal artists create the same scenes on canvases. People spend thousands of dollars to buy them. What are these paintings? Why are they so popular?

The art is known as "dreamtime" painting. The artists paint in dots instead of long brushstrokes. They use bright colors.

To an outsider, the paintings look like beautiful patterns and shapes. To the artists, they tell stories. The stories are about the creation of the world.

Many Aborigines believe that the world was created by spirit ancestors. These spirits lived long ago during dreamtime. They traveled across the globe. As they moved, they carved out the features of the earth. A serpent ancestor slithered. He left a river behind. A kangaroo ancestor thumped his tale. He made a lake.

In the 1970s, these dreamtime paintings were discovered by the art world. By the 1990s, people spent $120 million a year on Aboriginal art.

Some of the most famous works now sell for more than $100,000.

The artists don't always profit. Most of the money often goes to art dealers. In July 1997, a painting sold for $206,000. The artist's name was Johnny Warangkula Tjupurrula. He made almost nothing from that sale. That's because he had sold it 30 years earlier. He got $150 for it back then. According to a friend, Johnny wasn't bitter. He was sad that the painting's owner didn't share his love for the land.

This Aboriginal dreamtime painting shows the creation of Alice Springs in Central Australia. According to legend, the land was shaped by caterpillars, wild dogs, and other creatures.

Chapter Three

The Tribe That Hides from Man

In the early 1960s, the Panará people had never seen an airplane. They had never seen a car. They didn't know about telephones or television. They lived deep inside the rainforest in Brazil.

The Panará lived the way their ancestors had for centuries. The men fished. They used bows and arrows or clubs to hunt. The women gardened. They grew sweet potatoes and papaya. The tribe did not use money. They had no contact with the world outside the forest. They were known as "the tribe that hides from man."

One night in 1967, a small airplane appeared over the rainforest. Panará villagers looked up. Some thought the plane was a star falling from the sky. Others thought it might be invaders, so they shot arrows at it.

The airplane landed. It carried a team from Brazil's Indian Protection Service. The men had a message for the tribe.

The government was building a highway. It would be the first road through the rainforest. Its route ran right through Panará land.

South America

The Panará once lived deep within the tropical rainforests of Brazil. When the Brazilian government came to build a highway, they were moved to the Xingu Reserve.

Before long, more planes came. Huge trucks arrived to start work on the highway. The road workers brought diseases. The Panará got sick and many died. In two short years, disease killed off nearly the entire tribe. In the early 1970s, the Panará may have numbered as many as 800. By 1975, only 79 survived.

Chief Aká is one of the leaders of the Panará. He remembered the time well. "We were in our village and everybody began to die," he said.

"Others went deep into the woods, and more died. We were sick and weak and couldn't bury our dead."

The Brazilian government saw that the tribe might die out. So, they decided to move the Panará.

Eight years earlier, the tribe had seen their first airplane. Now, they had to ride in one. In 1975, they flew 250 miles west to the Xingu Reserve. Other tribes had already moved there. It was their only choice. Their land was quickly disappearing. Many tribes were in danger of dying off.

First Encounters

The story of the Panará really begins 500 years earlier. That's when European explorers first arrived in South America. Millions of Native Americans already lived on the continent. Some, like the Incas, built great civilizations. Still, their weapons were no match for the Spanish, who used cannons and guns. The explorers also brought deadly diseases. In a matter of decades, many tribes were wiped out.

In the 1500s, explorers from Portugal arrived in Brazil. A century later, they discovered gold. More settlers flocked to the area. A tribe called the Southern Cayapo (Kie-YAH-po) stood in their way.

The Southern Cayapo tried to resist the Portuguese settlers, but they fought a losing battle. By the early 1900s, settlers thought the tribe had died out.

They were wrong. A small band survived. This band was the Panará—the tribe that hides from man. They had moved deep into the forest. For many years, they avoided all contact with outsiders. Then, the road arrived.

Going Home

The move to the Xingu Reserve probably saved the Panará. Still, they weren't happy. On the reservation, land for farming was limited. Game was also **scarce**. The Panará moved around on the reservation. No place seemed right.

In the early 1990s, tribe members began to think about going home. Six Panará men went back to their old land. Most of the trees had been chopped down. The forest had been ruined. Only one part remained untouched. The trees there were still standing, and no one was living in the area.

"The land where I was born has been **consumed**," said Chief Aká. "White people can stay there and we won't argue. But we have found a part of our land that is still forest. We are going back there. If the white chiefs send their people there, we will fight."

In 1994, the Panará did fight back by filing a lawsuit. They insisted that part of the forest belonged to them. Many other Brazilians supported them. So did the court.

By 1998, the Panará had returned to their forest. Today, the tribe's lifestyle has changed. They hunt and farm, but they also watch satellite television. They wear shorts and dresses. They sell some of their goods for money.

The Panará still sing the old songs. They make the same meals their ancestors did. They try to hold onto the past. At the same time, the tribe is moving into the future.

When the Panará returned to their homelands, much of the forest had been burned and cut down. They built a new village on the one part that remained untouched.

Shrinking Forests

The Panará live in one of the earth's most valuable places. It's called the Amazon Rainforest. The Amazon is the largest rainforest on earth. The forest is spread out across nine different countries. Most of it lies inside the borders of Brazil. The rainforest once covered more than two million square miles. Now, it is disappearing fast.

Over the last 35 years, large sections have been destroyed. No one knows exactly how much. A group called the Rainforest Alliance works to save the forest. It says 6,000 square miles are lost every year. That's larger than the state of Connecticut!

The land is being cleared for profit. Ranchers want it for grazing. Farmers need it for growing crops. The timber industry cuts trees for lumber. Miners clear the land to dig mines.

As the forest disappears, tribes that live there are hurt. The Yanomami live not far from the Panará. They had almost no contact with outsiders until the 1980s. Then, gold was found on their land.

Miners flooded in. Nearly 2,000 Yanomami died from new diseases. In 1993, 19 more were murdered by miners. About 19,000 Yanomami still survive, but their culture may be dying fast.

Native cultures aren't the only valuable things being lost. Nearly *half* of Earth's life forms live in the rainforest. As the rainforest disappears, so do thousands of plant and animal species. About 130 species may die off every day!

Today, many groups like the Rainforest Alliance are fighting to save the rainforest. Some countries have passed laws to protect the land. Yet the forest keeps shrinking. Some people estimate that in 50 years it will all be gone.

Rainforest once covered much of South America. It may be disappearing at a rate of 6,000 square miles a year.

Glossary

Aborigine *(noun)* a European term for the native people of Australia

bias *(noun)* a prejudice; a leaning toward or against a group of people or point of view

casino *(noun)* a place for gambling

colonize *(verb)* to move into a new land and build settlements

consume *(verb)* to eat up or destroy

corrupt *(adjective)* bad or dishonest

debate *(verb)* to discuss or argue

federal *(adjective)* part of the national government

grievance *(noun)* a complaint

indigenous *(adjective)* native to an area

inferior *(adjective)* low in quality; second-rate

inform *(verb)* to teach or tell

loyalty *(noun)* true and faithful behavior

Index

Aborigines, 15–19, 20–21
Aká (chief), 24, 26
Amazon Rainforest, 28–29
American Indian Movement (AIM), 8–12
art, 20–21
Australia, 4, 5, 14–19

bias, 9
Brazil, 22, 24–26, 28

colonization, 5
cultures, 4–5, 8, 16–18, 20–21, 22, 26, 28–29

diseases, 5, 17, 24, 25, 28
dreamtime painting, 20–21

European settlers, 5, 6, 16–17, 24–25

gold, 6, 8, 25, 28

indigenous cultures, 4
indigenous people, 15, 18
inferior conditions, 9, 11, 25

loyalty, 14–15

Mabo, Eddie, 14–15, 18–19
Means, Russell, 8, 9, 10, 12
Mer Island, 14–15, 17, 18–19
minorities, 18

Native Americans, 6, 8–12, 13
Nixon, Richard, 11
North America, 4, 5, 6

Panará people, 22–26, 28

relocation, 6, 17, 24
reservations, 6, 8, 9, 25

Sioux, 6, 8, 9, 10
South America, 5, 24

Tecumseh, 13

Wounded Knee, 8, 9–11

Xingu Reserve, 24, 25

Yanomami tribe, 28–29

minority *(noun)* a group that is different from most of the people

nomadic *(adjective)* having a lifestyle in which you move from place to place

paradise *(noun)* a beautiful place that makes people feel happy and content

relocation *(noun)* the moving of a group or family to another area

reservation *(noun)* an area of land set aside for a special purpose, as for a tribe

resistance *(noun)* the refusal to accept something

scarce *(adjective)* hard to find; limited in supply

testify *(verb)* to give evidence in court

thriving *(adjective)* doing well or flourishing

Idioms

turn over *(page 8)* to give to someone else
They had to turn over their weapons.